A [illegible] Handwriting

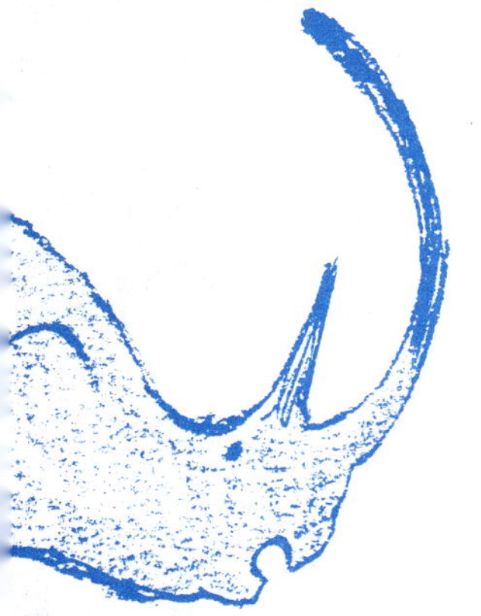

About 100 years ago the great Scottish essayist Thomas Carlyle declared, "Certainly the Art of Writing is the most miraculous of all things man has devised." Truer words were never written. Without writing, mankind would be forever in an aboriginal state with no way to pass knowledge from one generation to another.

Until 1994 it was believed that the oldest prehistoric cave paintings in southwestern France and northern Spain (Lascaux, Les Eyzies, Altamira, etc.) were created about 19,000 years ago. In 1994 new caves were discovered in southern France whose murals date from around 31,000 years ago, according to carbon-dating tests. The hordes of animals charging across the cave walls are not really writing and archeologists are not quite sure what they mean. But they are mankind's earliest graphic communication.

True writing didn't appear until around 5500 years ago when the inhabitants of the Tigris and Euphrates valleys developed ideographic symbols for whole words or phrases. The writing was called cuneiform because of the small wooden wedge (cuneus in Latin) used to press the symbols into a wet clay tablet. The tablet was then dried in the sun or fired in a small kiln. If the tablet isn't dropped it's one of the most permanent forms of writing ever developed. It didn't result in great literature but was the writing of ancient peoples such as the Assyrians, Babylonians and Persians for their invoices, bills of lading, ownership records, letters, etc.

The hieroglyphic (priestly) writing of the Egyptians is the outstanding script of the ancient world with its handsome pictorial ideographs standing for phrases, words, syllables and even individual letters. It

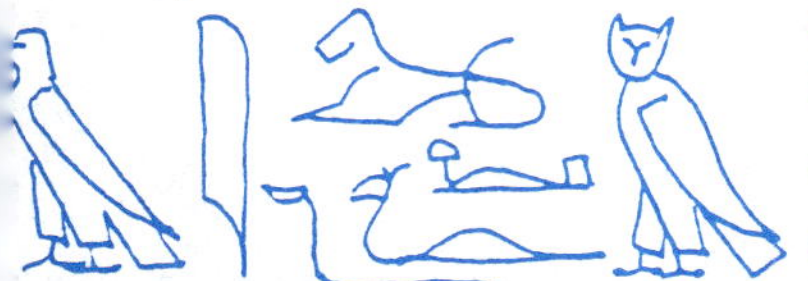

began early in the third millennium B.C. but was not deciphered until the early 19th century with the aid of the Rosetta stone. The Egyptians covered papyrus (ancestor of paper), wood, stone and ceramics with their decorative writing which often expressed prayers for the dead to facilitate their entry into the after life.

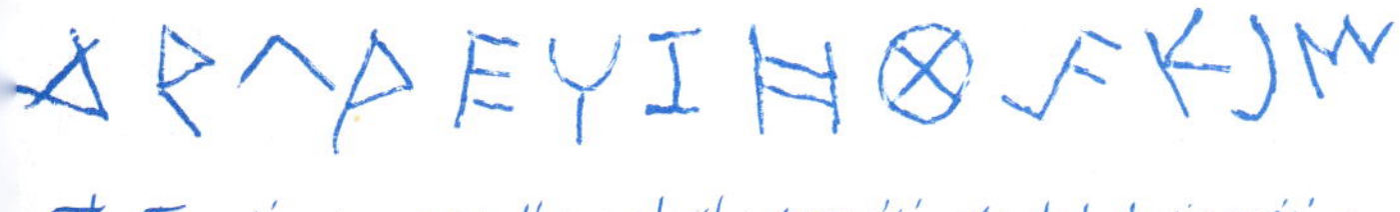

The Egyptians never really made the transition to alphabetic writing whose invention is generally credited to the Phoenicians around the 13th century B.C. They were entrepreneurs who lived in what is now Lebanon and traded with other peoples the length of the Mediterranean, going as far as present-day Portugal. The hieroglyphics were too cumbersome for the Phoenicians' commercial documents so they conceived the revolutionary [illegible] whole idea or word. It was a writing breakthrough [illegible] the invention of writing itself. The Phoenicians based the graphics of some of their letters on hieroglyphics but others look like Latin letters, largely because the Greeks borrowed heavily from the Phoenicians in developing the Greek alphabet. Then the Romans, who conquered the Greeks, took many Greek letters into the Latin alphabet, beautifying them with curves where the Greeks had used sharp angles. Strictly speaking, the Phoenicians had no vowels, using accent marks to indicate vowel sounds, and read right to left. The Greeks introduced vowel letters and finally changed the reading direction to left/right which succeeding European nations adopted.

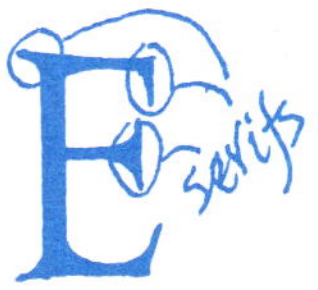

The Romans used the beautiful alphabet they perfected (and we inherited) to proclaim their conquests by having the messages carved in their triumphal arches. Read the description of Roman caps on the inside front cover (opposite). In the 2nd century B.C. in Phoenicia a substitute for papyrus was perfected – parchment, which is the skin of a small animal such as a lamb or a goat. It is smoother and more durable than papyrus and is very compatible to the quill pen which had replaced reed pens for writing. The quills were made (and still are) from the feathers of large birds such as geese, crows and turkeys. In fact, the word for pen in all western European languages (except English) is the same as feather. English 'pen' comes from Latin 'penna' – feather.

Read about Uncial, Caroline Miniscule and Gothic on the inside back cover. These predecessors to Chancery Cursive were lettering – not adaptable to handwriting. Scribes of the Italian 15th and 16th centuries perfected Italic Handwriting for inscribing papal 'bulls' or edicts. Since they were kept in the papal records office or chancery, the calligraphy was called Chancery Cursive. Its most influential practitioner was Ludovico degli Arrighi of Vicenza who published a 32-page manual in 1522 – La Operina (the little work), which has become the Bible of calligraphers even though Arrighi doesn't mention calligraphy. He was teaching 'la scrittura' – handwriting. In his book's foreword he hopes that his work will be of value not only to his age but to posterity as well.

la publica utilita e cómodo non ſolamente di questa etá, ma delli poſteri anchora, voleßi

Michelangelo wrote his poetry in Chancery. Elizabeth I wrote it well at 13. On the front cover border are other Renaissance greats and master calligraphers who've written it. Handwriting had a renaissance in the early 19th century with Spencerian and early 20th with Palmer. A new renaissance is sorely needed. Back to the future!

Published by La Stampa Calligrafica, Box 209, Franklin, MI 48025

ISBN 0-9606630-3-7

a BALL POINT PEN A

b is one stroke: aa abacadad aeaeafag ahaiaj Cap A is two strokes: B

c akalamanaoapaqaqar asasatauavawaxayaz Aa Ab Ac Ad Ae C

d ∂ is one stroke: bb babebebiblbobr buby Cap B is two strokes: D

e e abebebibobub Ba Be Be Bi Bl Bo Br Bu By E

f is one stroke: cc cacecicicocr cucy Cap C is one stroke: Ca Ce F

g acececicocu Ce Cl Co Cr Cu Cy G

h is one stroke: dd dadededido Terminal Cap D is two strokes H

ij dudy adededidodud adedediod ud Da De Do Dr Du IJ

k is one stroke or two: ee eaebeceded ef egeheiejekelemeneoepeqeq er es K

l esetеueveweх eyez eaebeceded efegeh Cap E is three strokes: L

m eiejekelemeneoepeq eqereseteuevewexeyez Ea Eb Ec Ed Ee Ef M

n is two strokes: ff fafefi fofr fs fu Cap F is three strokes: Fa Fe N

o af ef if of uf Fi Fl Fr Fu Fy O

p is one stroke: gg gagegeghgiglgo Cap G is one stroke: Ga P

Qq grgsgwgy ag egeg ig og ug Ge Gh Gl Gn Go Gr Gu Gy Q

r is one stroke: hh hahehehihohuhy Cap H is three strokes: R

s s ahehehuhohshthuhwh Ha He Hi Ho Hu Hy S

t is two strokes: ii iaibicidid ieiei fig ihij ikil Cap I is one stroke: T

u iminioipiqiq irisisitiuiviwixiyiz Ia Ic Id Ie Ie If Ig Ih Ik U

v is two strokes: jj ja je je ji jo ju Cap J is one stroke: Ja V

w aj ej ej ij oj uj Je Ji Jo Ju W

x is one stroke: kk kakekekikokuky Cap K is two strokes: Ka Ke X

y akekekikokuk Ke Ki Ko Ku Ky Y

z is one stroke: ll lalelelilolsluly Cap L is one stroke: La Le Le Z

12 alelelillolslul Lh Li Lo Lu Ly 78

34 is one stroke: mm mamememimoms Cap M is one stroke: Ma 9

56 mumy amememimom Page 2 Me Me Mi Mo Mr Ms Mu 0

BALLPOINT PEN

A
B
C
D
E
F
G
H
IJ
K
L
M
N
O
P
Q
R
S
T
U
V
W
X
Y
Z
78
9
0

a BALLPOINT PEN A

b is one stroke: nn nanenenq nnonsnsntnuny Cap N is one B

c anenenqninknonpnsnsnun Na Ne Ne Ni No stroke Nu C

d ∂ is one stroke: oo oaobocodoeofogohoiojokol Cap O is one D

ee omonoporosotouovowox oyoz aobocodoeofogo Oa Ob stroke: Oc E

f is one stroke: pp papbpdpepg phpiplpmpnpoppr Cap P is two F

g pspsptpupy apepepipopspup Pa Pe Pe Ph Pi Pl strokes G

h is two strokes or one: qu qu aq eq eq Cap Q is two strokes: H

ij iq oq uq aqeqeq oq uq Don't confuse q & g! Qu IJ

k is one stroke: rr rarererhrirorsrsrury ar br Cap R is two strokes: K

l or dr er er fr gr ir or pr sr sr tr ur wr Ra Re Re Ri Rh Ru Ro Ry L

m is one stroke, two forms: ss sascsesesesh sisk Cap S is one stroke: M

n slsmsnsospsqsrstsusvswsy ssasbscsds Sa Se Sh Si Sk Sl Sm N

o eses fs gshsisjskslsmsnsosrsusys zs Sn So Sp Sr O

p is two strokes: tt tatethtotrts ttutwtytz Cap T is two strokes: P

qg atetitotststut th or th Use the crossbar to connect! Ta Te Th Ti To Tr Q

r is one stroke: uu uaucuduèueueufuguhuiukul Cap U is one stroke R

ss umunuoupurusus utuwuw aubucuduèueufugu Ua Uc Ud Ue Ul S

t is one stroke: vv vavevwovrvy Cap V is one stroke: T

u avev evwovw Keep v and u distinct! Va Ve Ve Vi Vo Vu U

v is one stroke: ww wawewhwiwowrws Cap W is one stroke: V

w wy awew ewiwowswtw Wa We We Wi Wo Wr Ws W

x is two strokes: xx xa xexixoxuxy Cap X is two strokes: X

y axexixoxux Xa Xe Xe Xi Xo Xu Xy Y

z is one stroke: yy yayeyeyiyoyu Cap Y is two strokes: Ya Z

12 ay by cy dy ey ey iy ky ly my oy ry sy sy ty Ye Ye Yi Yo Yu 78

34 is one stroke: zz za ze ze zi zo zu Cap Z is one stroke: 9

56 az ez ez iz oz tz uz Page 4 Za Ze Zi Zo Zu 0

BALLPOINT PEN

A
B
C
D
E
F
G
H
IJ
K
L
M
N
O
P
Q
R
S
T
U
V
W
X
Y
Z
78
9
0

a FINE-POINT STUB PEN A

b Start with practicing the basic strokes of the calligraphy pen B

c with the point at a 45° angle to the paper: thin going up, thick C

dd coming down, lumps and loops — all at the 9° slant to the right: D

ee write over these { vvvvvvvvvvvvvvvvvvvvvvvvvvvvvvvvvvvvvvvv E

f mmmmmmmmmmmmmmmmmmm eeeeeeeeeeeeeeeeeeeeeeeeeeeeeee F

g Start writing here, copying over the model Italic Handwriting. G

h Start a is still a one-stroke letter: aaaaaa abacadad aeae afag ahai H

ij a aj akalamaanaoapaqaq ar asasatauavawax ay az IJ

k bacadaeaea fagahiajakalamanaoapaqaqarasasatauavawaxa K

l ya za Cap A is two strokes: Aa Ab Ac Ad Ae Af Ag Ah Ai Aj Ak Al L

m start A Am An An Ao Ap Aq Aq Ar As At Au Av Aw Ax Ay Az M

n In great attempts it is glorious even to fail! — Longinus N

o Start O

p b is one stroke: bbb ba bbebebiblbobr Cap B is two strokes: P

qq bsbsbuby abebebibobub BaBeBeBiBl B BoBrBuBy Q

r Progress is the mother of problems. R

ss variant S

t Start c is one stroke: ccccc cacecechcickcl Cap C is the same C T

u cocr cscsctcucy acecécicocuc Ca Ce Ch Ci C Cl Co Cu Cr C U

v Creditors have better memories than debtors. — Benjamin Franklin V

w W

x Start d is one stroke: dd dadededidodrdsdsdudwdy adededidod X

y d ud The terminal ∂ is one stroke or two: Start ∂ ∂ ad ed ed id Y

z Cap start D is two strokes: Da De De Di Do Du od ud pd Z

12 Dy Seize this very minute! What you can do, or 78

34 think you can do, begin it! — Goethe 9

56 0

FINE-POINT STUB PEN

A
B
C
D
E
F
G
H
IIJ
K
L
M
N
O
P
Q
R
S
T
U
V
W
X
Y
Z
78
9
0

Unlike the ballpoint pen, there is a definite relationship between pen width and letter height in Chancery Cursive with the stub pen — 5 pen widths 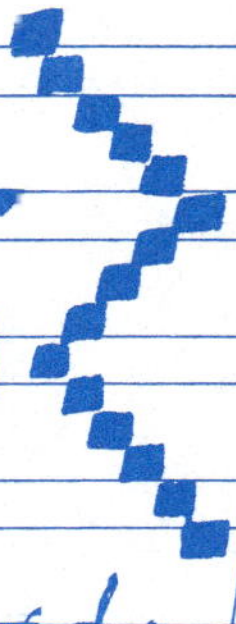 for lower case, 7½ for caps and certain figures (except for caps which dip below the line), 10 for ascenders, the same for descenders and 15 for the only lower-case ascender-descender — f; t rises about 1½ pen widths above the line and q and z go about 2½ below. However, the basic height relationships of lower case to caps, ascenders and descenders are the same for the ballpoint and the stub pen. (The large letters which start each alphabet section do not conform to these proportions).

aAdfqt5

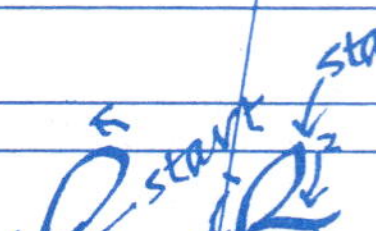

is one stroke or two, depending largely on how it connects with other letters: eee eaebecedeeef egeheiej ekel emeneoepeqeqer esesetenevewexeyez eee eaebecedeeefegehei ej ekelemeneoepeqeqer ese s eteuevewexeyez aebecedefegeheieje kelemeneoepeqeqeresesetenevewexeyeze aebecedefegeheiejeke lemeneoepeqeqeresesetenevewexeyeze. The two-stroke e is often used at the end of a word. Cap E is three strokes and uses its crossbar to connect with most of the letters that follow

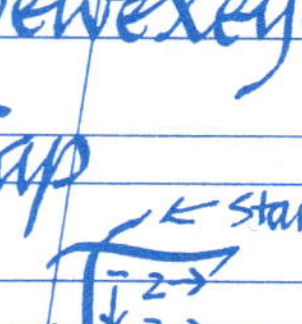

Ea Ec Ed Ef Eg Ei Ej Em En Eo Ep Eq Eq Er Es Et Eu Ev Ew Ex Ey Ez

The writings of the wise are the only riches our posterity cannot squander. — Walter Savage Landor

Try writing a sentence in which every word starts with an e.

FINE-POINT STUB PEN

A
B
C
D
E
F
G
H
IJ
K
L
M
N
O
P
Q
R
S
T
U
V
W
X
Y
Z
78
9
0

f is two strokes of grace and beauty: ff fa fe fi fl fo fr fs fu fy ffi af ef ef if of uf. Note how the crossbar connects with the following letter. Cap F F is three or two strokes.

Fa Fe Fi Fo Fr Fu Fy F Fa Fe Fi Fo Fr Fu Fy

Never judge a work of art by its defects. — Oscar Wilde

g is one stroke and doesn't connect with a following letter: g g g g ga ge ge gh gi gl gn go gr gs gs gu gw gy but it can join with letters that precede: ag eg eg ig ng og ug Cap G is one stroke but a graceful second stroke can be added

Ga Ge Gi Gn Go Gu Gw Gh Gl Ga Ge Gi Gn Go Gu Gw G

Success covers a multitude of blunders. — George Bernard Shaw

h is one stroke and connects easily with letters that follow: ha he he hi ho hs hs hu hy ah ch eh eh ih kh oh ph sh sh th th th uh wh

Practice th th both ways. Cap H H is three strokes with the crossbar joining the following letter: Ha He Hi Hu Hy

Art, like morality, consists in drawing the line somewhere.

— Gilbert K. Chesterton

i is two strokes, counting the dot; it's friendly with most letters — fore and aft: ii ia ib ic id id ie ie if ig ih ij ik il im in io ip iq iq ir is is it iu iv iw ix iy iz ai bi ci di ei ei fi gi hi ji ki li mi ni oi pi qi qi ri si si ti ui vi wi xi yi zi Cap I is three strokes with the bottom serif connecting to some letters: Ia Ic Id Ie Ig Im In Io Ip Ir Is It Iu Iw Iy

J is a one-stroke variant: Ja Jc Jd

FINE-POINT STUB PEN

A
B
C
D
E
F
G
H
IJ
K
L
M
N
O
P
Q
R
S
T
U
V
W
X
Y
Z
78
9
0

Ie If Ig Ih Ik Il Im In Io Ip, etc. It must not resemble a cap J! It's not enough that we do our best; sometimes we have to do what's required.
— Winston Churchill

j is two strokes, like i: jj jajejijojujy ajejej ij oj uj; note that the dots for j and i are like apostrophes. Cap J has a noble sweep in its single stroke: Ja Je Jg Jr Jo Ju Ji

To affect the quality of the day, that is the highest of arts. — Thoreau

k is one stroke. When its tail does not connect with the following letter, it can sweep below the line: kk kakakekekekekekhkhki kiklklklkokokr kr kukukyky akckekekikskuk Cap K's tail can either connect with the next letter or sweep under it. Cap K is two strokes. Ka Ka Ke Ke Ke Ke Ko Ko Ki Ki Kl Kl Ku Ku Ky Ky No person will have occasion to complain of the want of time who never loses any. — Thomas Jefferson

l is one stroke and likes its neighbors on both sides: ll lalblele lilklllolslsluly alclelelflglilklolplslslul Cap L is one stroke and snuggles under succeeding letters but does not connect with them: La Le Le Li Lo Lu Ly La belle écriture demande un esprit gai pour son execution. (Beautiful handwriting demands a lively spirit for its execution.) — French maxim

m is one stroke. Keep the humps nice and round: mm mame memimmomrmsmsmsmtmumy amememimosmsmum

FINE-POINT STUB PEN

A
B
C
D
E
F
G
H
IJ
K
L
M
N
O
P
Q
R
S
T
U
V
W
X
Y
Z
78
9
0

Cap M is one stroke and flows easily into succeeding letters: Ma Mc Me Me Mi Mo Mr Ms Ms Mu My An extra serif can be added: M Mr Ms The great consulting room of a wise man is a library. —Dawson

n is a one-stroke half m: nn nandnd neneng ninknonsns ntnuny anenenengninonpnsnsnyn When n or m finishes a word it can be extended: when seen am Cap N is one stroke: N Na Ne Ni No Extra strokes can be added: N N N N The most effective way to cope with change is to help create it. —L.W. Lynett

o can be made with one stroke or two. With two it is not practical to connect with the following letter: oaobocod od oeofogohoioj okolomonopoqoqovosotouovowoxoyoz aobocodo eoeofogohiojokolomonopoqoqovosotouovowoxoyozo Cap O takes two strokes: Oa Ob Oc Od Oe Oe Of Og Oh Oi Oj Ok But you can make it in one if you're in a hurry! Who makes quick use of the moment is a genius of prudence. —John Lavater

p is one stroke: pp papepephpiplpr pspsptpu apepepipopspspup Cap P is two strokes: Pa Pd Pe Pe Ph Pi Pl Po Pr Ps Ps Pt Pu
Genius is born, not paid. —Oscar Wilde

Q has two versions, one with two strokes, the other with one: Q Q qu qqu aqeqeq aquequequ Be sure this q isn't a g!

FINE-POINT STUB PEN

A
B
C
D
E
F
G
H
IJ
K
L
M
N
O
P
Q
R
S
T
U
V
W
X
Y
Z
78
9
0

b Cap Q is three strokes. Handwriting is jewelry fashioned by the B
c Qu hand from the pure gold of the intellect. — al-Tawhidi (10c) C
dd D

ee r is one stroke and connects with the following letter only when E
f writing fast: rr ra re rer hr ir or r rs rs r tr ur y ar br cr dr er er fr gr ir F
g kr or pr sr sr tr ur wr Cap R R can have a short or long G
h tail, both two strokes: Ra Re Re Ri Ro Ru Ry Ra Re Rh Ri H
ij The moving finger writes; and having writ, moves on. — Omar Khayyám IJ
k K

l s has two one-stroke versions, whose choice may vary according L
m to the letter that precedes or follows: ss sa sc se se se sh si sl sm M
n sn so sp sr ss st su sv sw sy as bs cs ds es es fs gs hs is ks ls ms ns os ps qs rs ts us N
o vs ws xs ys zs ss sa sc se se sh si sk sl sm sn so sp sq sr st su sv sw sy sz as bs O
p ds es es fs gs hs is js ks ls ms ns os ps rs ts us vs ws xs ys zs ss or ss Cap S P
Qq has only one version and one stroke: Sa Sc Se Se Sh Si Sk Sl Q
r There's nothing worth the wear of winning but laughter and R
ss the love of friends. — Hilaire Belloc S
t T

u t is two strokes with the crossbar connecting wherever U
v possible with letters that follow: tt ta te th ti to tr ts tt tu tw ty V
w tz at ct et ft gt it ot st st st ut xt zt Cap T is also two strokes: W
x Ta Te Te The Ti To Tu Tw Ty Time is the most X
y valuable thing a man can spend. — Theophrastus Y
z Z

12 u is one stroke and very friendly to letters that precede or follow: 78
34 uu ua ub uc ud ue ue uf ug uh ui uj uk ul um un uo uq ur us us ut uw 9
56 0

FINE-POINT STUB PEN

A
B
C
D
E
F
G
H
IIJ
K
L
M
N
O
P
Q
R
S
T
U
V
W
X
Y
Z
78
9
0

uvuwuxuyuz aubucuduеueufuguhuiujukulumunuoupququru susutuvuwuxuyuzu Cap U is the same as the lower-case u and also connects with the following letter: Ua Ub Uc Ud Ue Ue Uf Ug Uh Ui Uj Uk Ul Um Un Uo Up Uq Uq Ur Us Us Ut Uv Uw Ux Uy Uz We take no note of Time but from its loss. — Edw. Young

v is one stroke and connects with letters on both sides: vv va vevivovu avevivovuv Bring the bottom to a point!

Cap V is a twin: Va Ve Ve Vi Vo Vu An artist's career always begins tomorrow. — Whistler

w is one stroke and likes its neighbors left and right: ww wa wewhwiwowr wswu awewgwiwowswtwuw Cap W is also one stroke: Wa We We Wh Wi Wo Wr

I am a galley slave to pen and ink! — Balzac

x is two strokes. The second stroke may have to be made after the word is finished: exit. xx xaxexexixoxu axexexix oxuxxx Cap X is also two strokes: Xa Xe Xe Xi Xo Xu Certainly the Art of Writing is the most miraculous of all things man has devised. — Thomas Carlyle

y is one stroke and joins only preceding letters: yy yayeyeyiyoys ysyu ay by cy dy ey ey iy ly oy sy sy uy wy zy Cap Y is the same one-stroke letter: Ya Ye Ye Yi Yo Yu Love is not love which alters when it alteration finds. — Wm. Shakespeare

FINE-POINT STUB PEN

A
B
C
D
E
F
G
H
IJ
K
L
M
N
O
P
Q
R
S
T
U
V
W
X
Y
Z
78
9
0

Z (start) is one stroke and difficult to connect with another letter except a preceding o or t: zz za ze zi zo zu az ez ez iz oz tz uz. Cap Z (start) is also one stroke: Za Ze Ze Zi Zo Zu Zy

Fine writing is next to fine doing. — Keats

Unlike the ballpoint calligraphy, the figures in stub-point Chancery have ascenders and descenders. The former go to cap height and the latter to about the same distance below the line:

1 2 3 4 5 7 9 6 8 8 0 “ ” ! ? & : ; . ,

123790 and one version of 8 are one stroke, 4,5 and the other 8 are two strokes. These are called 'old-style' figures.
Quotes and apostrophe are cap height “ ” ' as are ! ? &. $ is big or little $. 'Calligraphy' means 'beautiful writing' in Greek.

Signor Arrighi did not lay down rigid rules for connecting letters, leaving the option to those who adopted his handwriting. As the distinguished American calligrapher, Raymond F. DaBoll, advised, “Calligraphy, like any other form of democracy, is controlled freedom.” But remember — connect letters; write, don't print!

After you've practiced with your Sheaffer Calligraphy pen you can go back to your ballpoint and make your caps and figures more calligraphic: ABCDEFGHIJKLMNOPQRTUVWYZ1234567890
Now that you have the basics of this beautiful and legible Italian Renaissance hand under your fingertips, use it whenever you write. Practice with, “The quick brown fox jumps over the lazy dog.” As Arrighi might have wished you, “Buona fortuna!” (Good luck).

FINE-POINT STUB PEN

A
B
C
D
E
F
G
H
IJ
K
L
M
N
O
P
Q
R
S
T
U
V
W
X
Y
Z
78
9
0

Let's have some fun with 'live' letters. Make the body of the creature with the Sheaffer pen and the arms, legs, wings, heads, feet and other parts that are not the basic letter with your ballpoint pen.

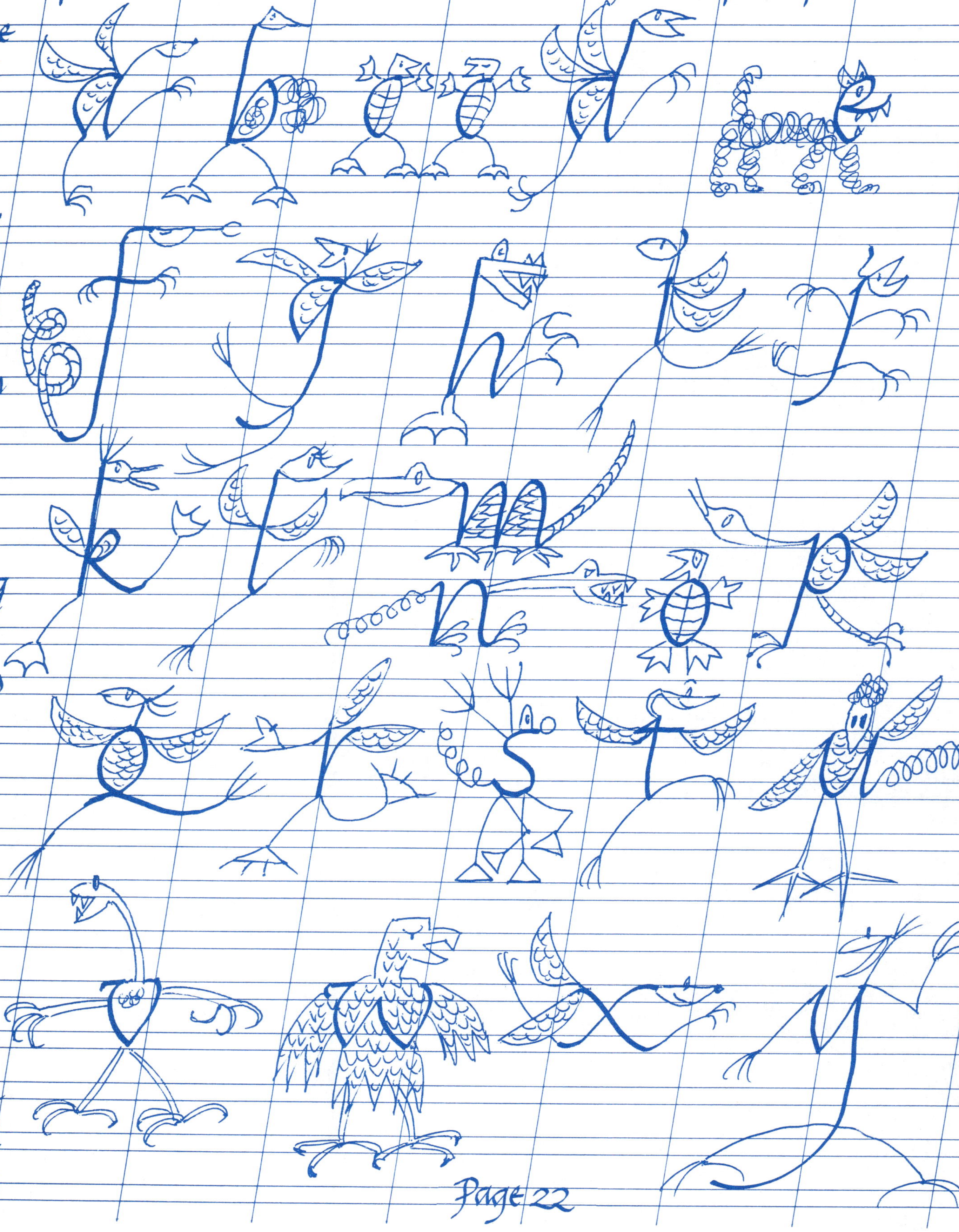

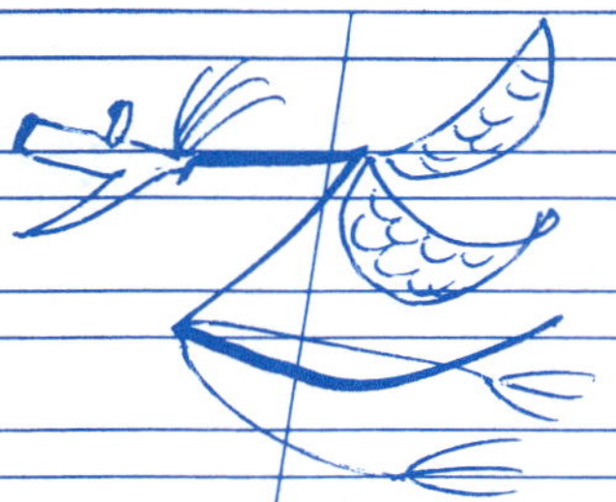

Instead of writing over the live letters on page 22, copy them on this page and create some of your own like the ones below. You may need more paper. Enjoy bringing letters to life!

a and z don't like each other because they never touch.

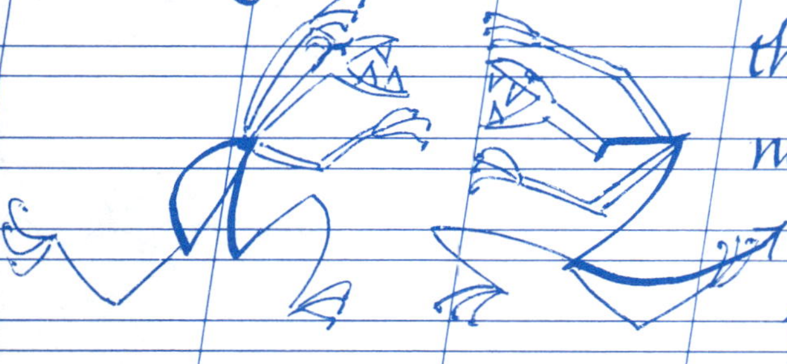

e and d are very much in love.

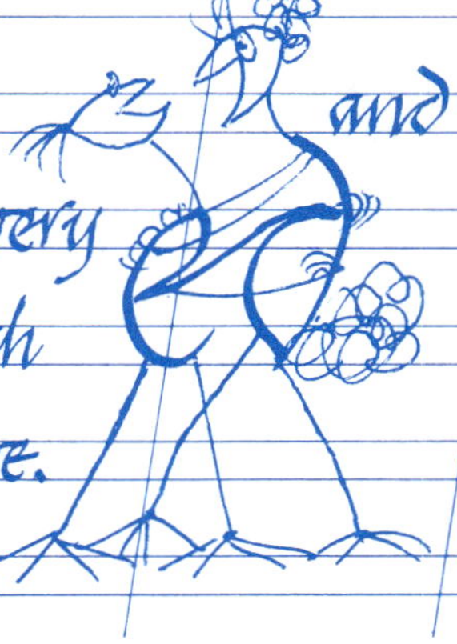

A B C D E F G H IJ K L M N O P Q R S T U V W X Y Z 78 9 0

Until Johannes Gutenberg invented movable type in the early 15th century, all books were laboriously calligraphed by hand on vellum—one letter at a time. Here in a medieval scriptorium is a monk calligraphing a book. The volumes around him he uses for reference in his copying.

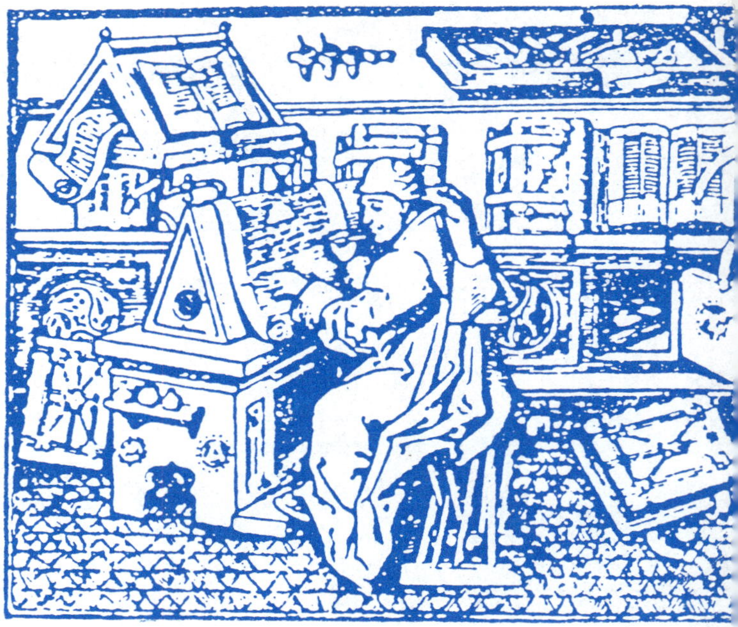

Helpful Hints

1. Speedy handwriting is the enemy of legibility. The mind makes words faster than the hand can write them. So start slowly and carefully. As your skill develops you'll be able to write as fast as you did with your old handwriting—and more beautifully and legibly!
2. When you're copying the lines from the left-hand pages onto the right-hand pages try hard to fit your copied lines into the same space as they took on the left-hand page. If your handwriting doesn't fit, don't carry letters over to the next line. Start each copied line fresh.
3. Your Sheaffer Calligraphy pen will give you many Chancery letters. You can replace it at your office supply store where you can also buy cartridges in a variety of colors and a set with 3 pen barrels, 3 assorted-width nibs and 14 cartridges in assorted colors.
4. La Stampa offers an English-made Platignum Starter Set with 4 different-width nibs, 2 black ink cartridges and a rubber vacuum-fill bulb for the pen barrel. Price: $8.95 including shipping and tax (see address pg. 1). Either the Sheaffer or the Platignum calligraphy fountain pen will divorce you from the loops of Palmer cursive handwriting that descended from early 19th century Spencerian. Become a born-again Italic Handwriter!
5. La Stampa also offers a 48-page blue-lined practice pad 8½x11 with the lines spaced the same as in this manual. Price $4, shipping and tax included. Blue lines disappear in Xeroxing.
6. If you decide to become a born-again handwriter and change your signature to Italic Handwriting, just inform La Stampa Calligrafica and you will be promptly enrolled in the American Society for the Diminution of Ugly and Illegible Handwriting (no dues) and you'll receive your membership certificate. Legally all you have to do is sign new bank account and voting registration cards. It's very simple. The author of this manual did it 40 years ago!